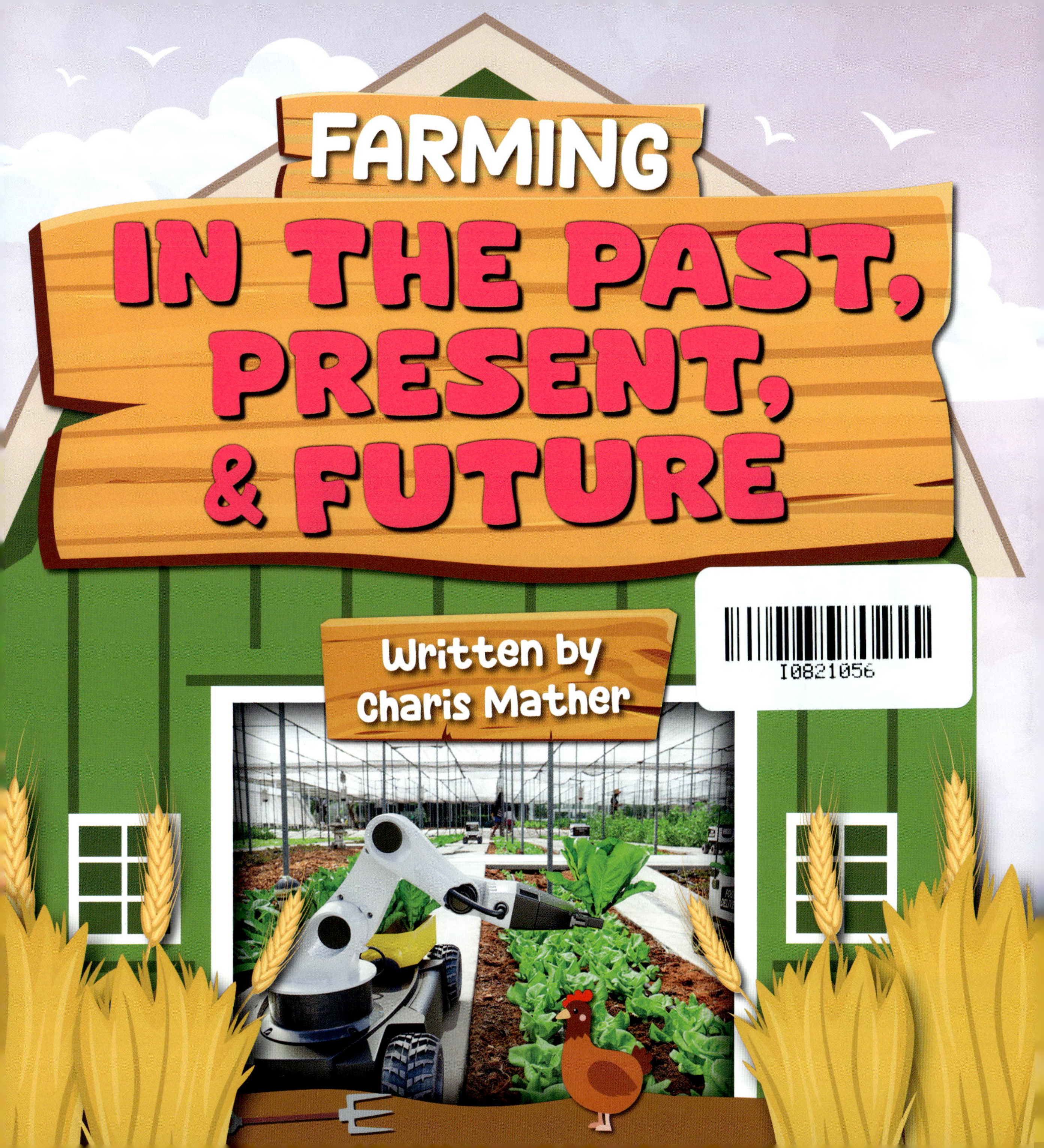
FARMING
IN THE PAST,
PRESENT,
& FUTURE
Written by
Charis Mather
I0821056

Library of Congress Control Number:
The Library of Congress Control Number is available on the Library of Congress website.

ISBN
979-8-89359-423-2 (library bound)
979-8-89359-443-0 (paperback)
979-8-89359-482-9 (epub)
979-8-89359-463-8 (hosted ebook)

Printed in the United States of America
Mankato, MN
012026

sales@northstareditions.com
888-417-0195

Written by:
Charis Mather

Edited by:
Noah Leatherland

Designed by:
Ker Ker Lee

Image Credits – Images courtesy of Shutterstock.com, unless otherwise stated.

Cover & Recurring – Ysami, Belozer, PCPartStudio, yusufdemirci, Tatiana Vizir, Alyona, Anatolir, Hybrid_Graphics, NanoAgency, MN Studios, Suwin66, Joann Vector Artist. 4–5 – maxim ibragimov, Everett Collection, 1st footage. 6–7 – Vladimir Melnik, mountainpix. 8–9 – Yarikart, Ole Dor, alexkich, Budimir Jevtic. 10–11 – Stephen William Robinson, Claudia Harms-Warlies, GLF Media, NOWRA photography, Stephen William Robinson. 12–13 – fotorince, Alexander Raths. 14–15 – Bits And Splits, WESTOCK PRODUCTIONS. 16–17 – Thanakorn.P, GreenOak, Victor Moussa. 18–19 – Ground Picture, BearFotos. 20–21 – Bannafarsai_Stock, mongione. 22–23 – Dmytro Surkov. kung_tom.

CONTENTS

Words that look like <u>this</u> can be found in the glossary on page 24.

FARMING IS FASCINATING

The way people farm has changed over time. Many modern farms use technology. Farming has become faster. New technology is often based on the tools and practices of the past.

The more farmers learn, the better they can make their farms. They need to understand a lot about science, their equipment, and the environment. Farming is difficult, but it's also fascinating.

FARMING IN THE PAST

Domestication

Farming began with domesticating plants and animals. Humans started to use wild plants and animals for food, clothing, work, and other things.

To domesticate means to bring under human control Sheep and goats were among the first domesticated farm animals.

Work Animals

Early farmers used strong animals to help with difficult jobs. Cattle and horses were useful for breaking apart the soil. They also helped pull heavy equipment.

Simple Tools

Early farmers used their hands and simple tools. They planted seeds. They harvested small areas of land. Early tools were made from stone or wood. Later, tools were made from metal.

New Techniques

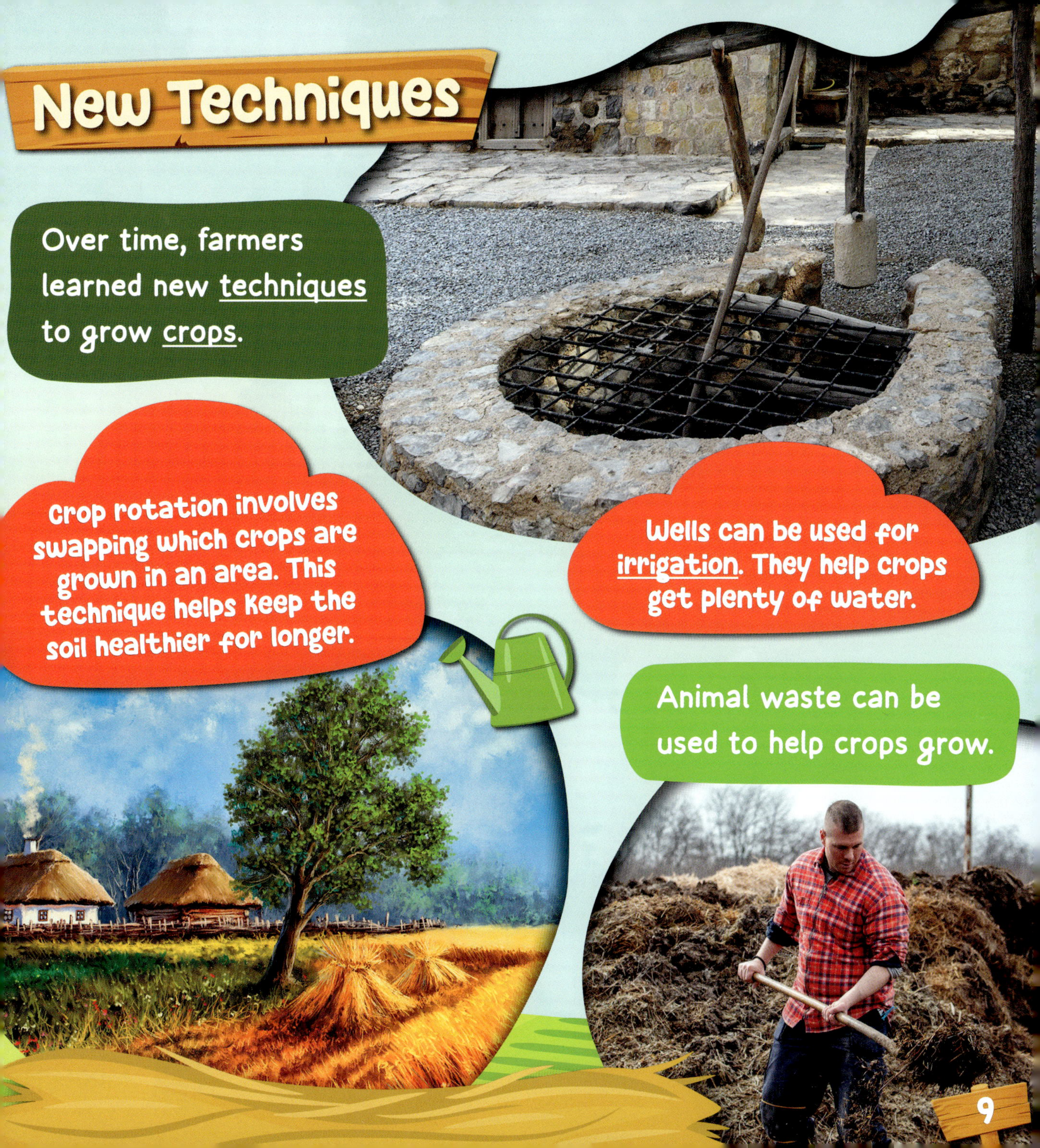

Over time, farmers learned new techniques to grow crops.

Crop rotation involves swapping which crops are grown in an area. This technique helps keep the soil healthier for longer.

Wells can be used for irrigation. They help crops get plenty of water.

Animal waste can be used to help crops grow.

FARMING IN THE PRESENT

Today, many small or traditional farms still use some of the same tools from the past. Other farms use new technology. These farms are bigger and more productive.

Today, farmers can grow crops in difficult environments. They can also use tools such as tractors and combines. Farmers can plant and harvest more than they could with the simpler tools of the past.

Selective Breeding

Selective breeding is one technique farmers use. Farmers choose the best crops or animals to make better seeds or young. They choose what to breed based on looks, taste, health, and more.

Too much selective breeding can be unhealthy for animals.

Selective breeding was once used on ancient farms. It has improved with modern science.

Now, scientists study plants and animals before farmers breed them. Then, they can get the best results.

FARMING IN THE FUTURE

In the future, farmers may need newer technology. Humans may invent techniques to solve problems that modern farmers face.

Farmers and scientists work to improve technologies and techniques. They want to help the farmers of the future.

Future Technologies and Techniques

Some farmers use small flying machines called drones to water crops and spread chemicals. It's estimated that farm drone use will increase in the future. This may save farmers money and time.

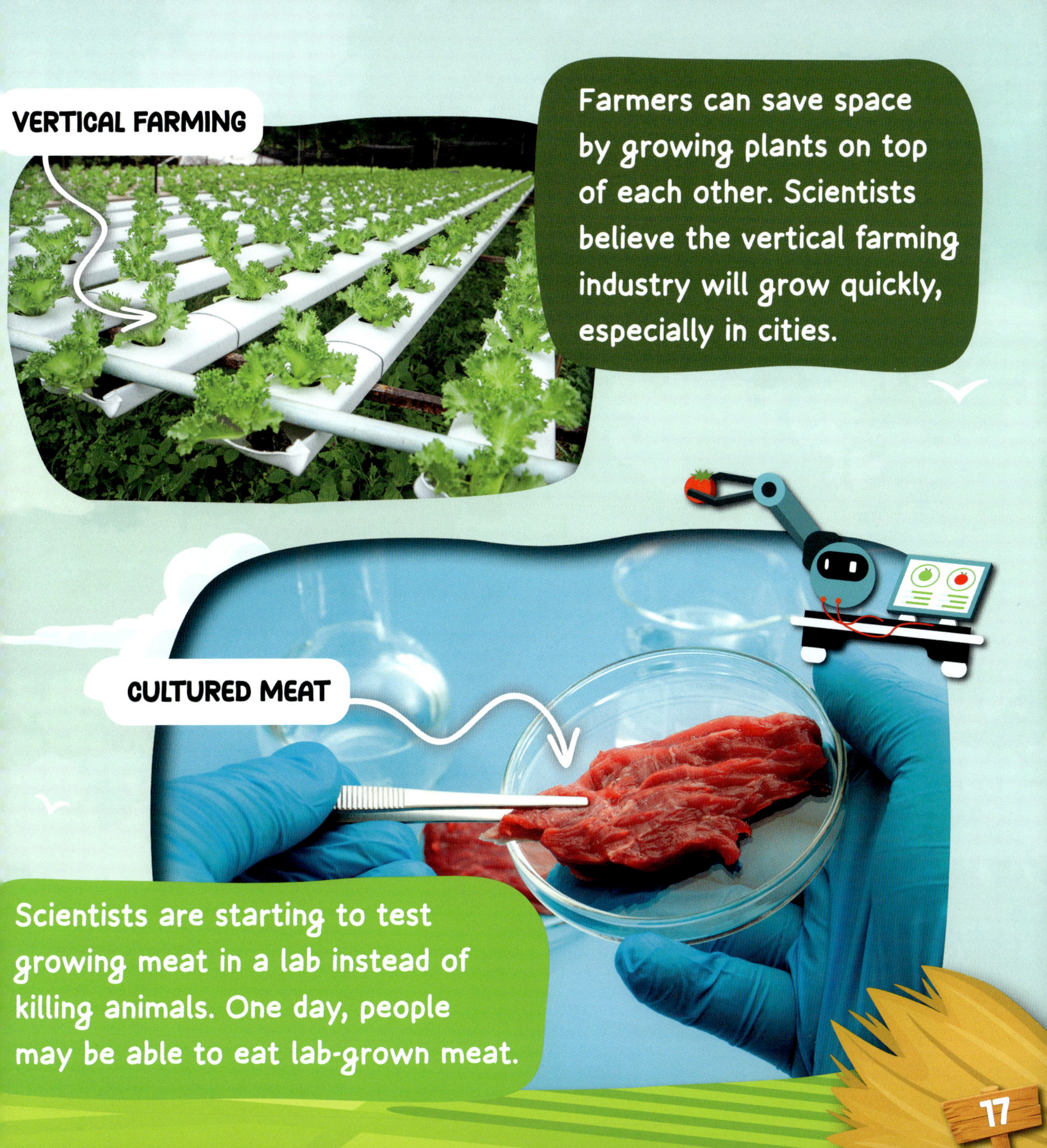

Farmers can save space by growing plants on top of each other. Scientists believe the vertical farming industry will grow quickly, especially in cities.

Scientists are starting to test growing meat in a lab instead of killing animals. One day, people may be able to eat lab-grown meat.

FOOD FOR ALL

The number of humans on the planet is always growing. More and more people will need food. Farmers have always had to find ways to keep up with that growth.

Modern farming practices produce plenty of food. However, much of it is wasted or does not get to those who need it. Getting healthy food where it is needed is as important as farming it.

THOUGHTFUL FARMING

Farmers have always faced challenges. They deal with bad weather, insects, and disease. But they need to be thoughtful about how they solve these problems.

Some farming practices fix problems quickly. But then they cause other problems later. Chemicals can end up hurting the environment. Some practices make large amounts of food but are unfair to animals.

FARMING FOR A BETTER FUTURE

Farming is one of the world's oldest and most important jobs. Farmers have always had to work very hard to feed people.

Today's farmers continue to use science to change the way they farm. They might find some new practices and techniques. These could lead to a fantastic future of farming.

GLOSSARY

chemicals substances that can be added to a material to change something about it

crops plants that are grown on a large scale to be eaten or used

environment the natural world

harvested gathered crops

irrigation human-made systems that add water to crops

modern to do with recent or present times

productive able to make a lot of something

techniques ways of doing something

technology inventions or methods based on scientific understanding or knowledge

traditional to do with beliefs, customs, or ways of behaving that have been around for a long time

INDEX